Skip the Funeral

BY BILL GOLDSTEIN

The Goldstein Project
10 Masthead Lane
East Hampton, NY 11937
bill@billgoldstein.com
www.billgoldstein.com

Ordering Information:
Quantity sales. Special discounts are available on quantity purchases by corporations, associations, and others. For details, contact the permissions coordinator at the address above.
Orders by U.S. trade bookstores and wholesalers. Please contact Book Baby: Tel: (877) 961-6978 or visit www.bookbaby.com.

Printed in the United States of America

PREFACE

Between these covers you'll find musings about everyday life. Things that may lie just beneath your daily consciousness but that you will nevertheless recognize immediately. Varied as to form and content, these short bursts are not easily described collectively. For both my podcast "Not That You Asked" and website www.billgoldstein.com, we've settled on "Stories. Observations. Pet Peeves." A pretty fair description of *Skip the Funeral*, as well.

What are these musings about? One reviewer of "Not That You Asked" explained:

> "Anything. Everything. Things you may have wondered about. Or things you never in a million years have thought about but will now wonder why you haven't."

And if you should also find yourself occasionally nodding in agreement or saying to yourself, "Hmm, never thought of it that way," that would be lovely too.

Disclaimer: I have done my best to accurately re-create dialogue, though many of these conversations are not recent and have been drawn from my imperfect — and no doubt biased — memory. Still, as presented, these exchanges accurately represent the spirit of what was said, and how it was said.

1

SKIP THE FUNERAL

"Goldstein, phone call," hollered one of my classmates. "Sounds like your old man."

It's the mid-'60s and I'm a freshman at the University of Rochester, 400 miles from my parents' home outside Boston. Long-distance telephoning was expensive, so calls from home were rare and therefore alarming, especially one from my father. I rushed to the phone assuming bad news.

"Pa, everything alright?" I asked nervously.

"Yes, son, everything's just fine. I'm calling to tell you we're planning an 85th birthday party for your grandfather. You're a busy boy these days, so I wanted to let you know right away. It's six weeks from next Saturday, plenty of time for you to sort out your schedule. I know you'll want to be here."

My grandfather, Maurice "Mosey" Goldstein, was an immense, bighearted man and a stalwart of his community. Legend has it (as a boy I heard this story many times from many different people, though never from my grandfather or my father) that as a young man Mosey physically intervened on behalf of an elderly Hasid being pulled off a milk truck and dragged by his beard along the street by a local, Jew-hating street tough. As the story goes, the cretin went down hard... and never got up.

ROUGH HEWN AND SQUARE-SHOULDERED, HE WAS AS TOUGH AS A $2 STEAK.

Mosey could drink everyone under the table while remaining sober as a judge. It was as if he had a cotton leg. Started each day at 4:30am with "a smile," the quaint term of yesteryear for a shot of whisky — in his case, two bracing ounces of Teacher's, neat, on his way out the door to Boston's wharf, where he bought fish every morning for his kosher fish market on Blue Hill Avenue in Roxbury. Pity the customer who made the mistake of asking if the fish was fresh, an insult that would trigger an exceedingly stern rebuke.

A first-generation American, Mosey worked hard and dreamed big. His two sons, my father and my uncle Sam, were never allowed to so much as cross the threshold into his market, permitted only to make deliveries during the busy High Holidays. He wanted better for his sons and he succeeded. Both graduated from Boston Latin School and later from Harvard and MIT respectively.

Even after he retired, at age 91, Mosey still lived in Roxbury in the same 5th-floor walkup he'd occupied for decades despite the neighborhood having long since morphed from working-class Jewish into dangerous ghetto. Mosey wouldn't budge.

This was a man who in 1898, at the age of 17, tricked his father — fluent in Yiddish only — to sign his official-looking Army enlistment papers by telling him that he was applying for a job with the Post Office. Eight weeks later he was in Cuba with Teddy Roosevelt and the Rough Riders fighting in the Spanish-American War, the first time Americans fought on foreign soil. The war lasted only 124 days but had substantial historical significance — largely unrecognized — forcing Spain to not only release Cuba from 400 years of colonial rule but also cede Puerto Rico, Guam, and the Philippines to the U.S. (for but $20 million total), all of which confirmed the U.S. as a global power.

"They called us Rough Riders, but when we shipped out of Tampa to Santiago there was no room for most of our horses and mules, which were left behind. When we took San Juan Hill, TR was on a horse all right, but I was in the mud, on foot like almost all the rest of us so-called Rough Riders."

Like 80% of the troops, Mosey came back to the States with yellow fever and nearly died at Camp Wikoff, a 5000-acre quarantine camp hastily constructed on the barren, uninhabited plains of Montauk on the tip of Long Island (not quite so barren these days), where more men perished than were lost in Cuba. Thankfully, Mosey recovered and was eventually sent home, in the process qualifying for an Army disability pension he would collect for the next 80 years.

MY KNEES BUCKLED FROM THE IMPACT OF HIS QUESTION.

Roughhewn and square-shouldered, he was as tough as a $2 steak, and even at 90 would not hear of plans to relocate from his beloved Roxbury neighborhood.

> "This is my home. Has been for 90 years. No one's gonna bother me here," he'd bark at my father with unshakable confidence. "Save your breath. I ain't movin'."

And he never did.

Mosey also had a serious bias against mustaches, especially the one on the youngest of his six grandsons, and was always trying to buy it off me, creating jocular sparring whenever we were together.

"How much you want for that mess under your nose?" he'd noodge. "Here, here's a double sawbuck. Take a shave, will ya? No one trusts a man with a mustache. You look like the guy who ties little girls to the railroad tracks."

He was a one-off character, all right, and I was hugely fond of him, and — back to the phone call — replied enthusiastically to my father's announcement.

"Wonderful news. Just let me check my schedule and I'll get back to you right away."

"No, no," my father said resolutely, never one to tolerate needless delays. "Check now. I'll hold."

Dashing back to my room to look at my calendar, I discovered a serious problem. With immense hesitancy I returned to the phone and sheepishly explained:

"Pa, I can't believe it, but unfortunately I have a major league conflict. That's the biggest social weekend of the year. The fraternity I'm pledging is having a huge party and I'm expected to be there. Plus I have a date with a girl I've been chasing since I got here. I'm really, really sorry, but I don't see how I can make it."

My father was not an explosive man, rarely raising his voice. But he could be seriously sarcastic. He waited for a few long seconds and then finally asked:

"Tell me, fraternity boy, when your grandfather dies, will you make time to come to his funeral?"

My knees buckled from the impact of his question.

"Pa, how could you ask me that? Of course I'll come to Grandpa's funeral."

"Well, I'll tell you what."

He paused for emphasis, then slowly instructed,

"Skip the funeral. Come to the party. You won't be able to give your grandfather a hug or let him know how much you love him at his funeral. Honor him while he's alive, son."

Well, I went to that birthday party, and was profoundly glad that I did. A dozen years later, I bore witness at my grandfather's funeral, too, ever thankful that I'd been set straight about priorities years earlier. Hot date notwithstanding.

2

HUMILIATION

I started working at Madison Square Garden in 1974 — my first job in
sports.

LEGENDS BEGAN TO POPULATE THE TABLE.

One afternoon, about a month in, I was invited to attend a black-tie
sports awards banquet later that very night, for which the Garden had
bought a table. There'd been a late cancellation and someone suggested
inviting the "new kid lawyer" to see how he'd handle himself. I had no
idea who else would be at the table and was told only:

"Bring your A game."

I was ecstatic, all but levitating. Dashing out to rent a tux and get my
shoes shined, I arrived at the Waldorf just in time for the beginning of

the cocktail hour.

These black-tie dinners are nonstop booze fests. Open bar during an overly long cocktail reception, followed by wine and hard liquor flowing all night long at each table. Recklessly, I overdid it during the reception, two-fistedly drinking like the young fool I was. By the time I took my seat early at the Garden's table, I was half in the bag, waiting expectantly to see who would fill out the table.

To my amazement, one by one, legends began to arrive: master impresario Sonny Werblin; Garden president and dashing man about town Mike Burke; Ned Irish, founder of the New York Knicks; Red Holzman, Knicks head coach; basketball Hall of Famers Walt Frazier and Willis Reed; hockey Hall of Famers Rod Gilbert and Emile Francis; and Howard Berk, the Garden executive who'd invited me. In the ensuing decades, I would come to attend dozens of such dinners, though never one with more august tablemates.

As the guests arrived, fairly trembling I rose to introduce myself and was greeted by a succession of quizzical looks as each one tried to figure out what a pup like me was doing at this table. I was wondering the same thing.

Desperate to make an impression, I jumped right in when Werblin made a critical remark about the Designated Hitter rule then being proposed in baseball. Had I been more seasoned, never mind less inebriated, I would have held my tongue and not felt compelled to try to impress. But I was young and dumb and too eager, and leapt at the first chance to flap my gums.

"I agree, Mr. Werblin," as if he cared. "Adopting the DH would be an abomination, a perversion of the game," I blurted out, just getting warmed up.

THIS WAS A WORLD-CLASS DEBACLE.

In mid-rant, fingers jabbing, arms flailing, like a total bozo I sent a full glass of wine sailing across the table. Shattering as it landed on top of another glass, shards of glass and gobs of red wine spilling all over Ned Irish, the senior most person at the table. Apoplectic, apologizing profusely, I leapt to my feet to try and mop it all up. Mr. Irish was incredibly gracious, but this was a world-class debacle that no amount of generous pooh-poohing could mitigate.

After an uncomfortably long, pregnant pause, my night's sponsor, Howard Berk, who by now surely regretted having invited me, tersely summed up my maiden voyage into the deep end of the pool:

"An inauspicious beginning, to say the least."

I wanted to shoot myself.

In time I would climb out of that elephantine hole and go on to partner successfully with the Garden for the next 25 years on the Virginia Slims Tennis Championships, which grew into arguably the world's largest annual women's sports event. But that night you could have gotten long odds on my sports career lasting even another 25 days.

3

MANHATTAN

HERE'S A RIDDLE

What's the *one* thing you need to live contentedly in Manhattan?

No... not money. That's the B answer. Everyone struggles financially when they come to New York City. But if you possess the one indispensable thing you need, you're likely to make a go of it.

When I arrived in Manhattan, in 1974, the subway was a quarter. Still, I was so broke I walked everywhere. Saving a quarter bought me a street-vended hotdog with kraut for lunch. Eating on the cheap every day did not make me miserable, however, because I had the *one* thing you need to live contentedly in the Big Apple.

I had a good reason. The A answer.

The hard truth is, if you can do what you want to do elsewhere, as well as you can do it in Manhattan, you should do it elsewhere. Full stop.

Why? Because Manhattan exacts such a high toll on people that, without a good reason, in time that toll becomes untenable. Money makes it easier, of course, but everyone, no matter their resources, must contend with relentless daily pounding from the Big Apple. No one's immune to high winds when you're living in a hurricane.

SOME SAY NEW YORKERS ARE RUDE. THIS IS A CARELESS FICTION.

People here get up, go to work, come home, and at the end of the day wonder to themselves:

> "Why am I so damn tired? I didn't do anything especially taxing today. I just got up, went to work, and came home."

Yeah, but you did it in Manhattan, pal.

Studies confirm that Manhattanites walk faster, much faster, than people anywhere else in the world, though they're certainly not trying to win a contest with the citizens of Mexico City or Cairo or Beijing. They're just in a hurry, on the make, doing everything they can, as fast as they can, to succeed in a place packed with millions of others trying just as hard, maybe harder, to do the same thing.

Some say New Yorkers are rude. This is a careless fiction. New Yorkers are not rude. If you ask for directions from a New Yorker, you will almost certainly get a response without rudeness. But you've probably interrupted someone who's what? In a hurry. And now you've slowed them down. You'll still get your directions, all right, most probably exacting ones, too, but you may have to walk alongside them, at *their* pace, going in *their* direction, to get them. Plus they're not apt to ask where you're from, what you do, or how you like the City. They don't have the time or, dare I say, the interest. But this doesn't make them rude. Just preoccupied, desperate to fit 25 hours of hustling into a 24-hour day.

Manhattan is among the busiest, densest places on the planet. Dense with people, buildings, vehicles, noise and angst. But it's also dense with synapses and opportunity. There's simply more going on here, so naturally it's harder to make your mark. Just as a ringside seat costs more than one in the rafters, so too is peddling your papers in uber-competitive Manhattan more challenging than elsewhere.

However, if you have a good reason for being here, then the price is worth it: if, and only if, you're able to balance the equation between what you give up by residing and working here — ease of living — with what you get in return — uncommon opportunity. And you do that by aggressively exploiting the City's unique resources, which, after all, is why you came in the first place.

THERE WAS NO GOOD ANSWER.

But remember, the sands of time shift. You might have a good reason for slugging it out in Manhattan this year, but lose it next. Once you stop drafting off the unique resources of the City, the equation will become imbalanced and you'll be on your way to losing that good reason, and likely soon reduced to a dysfunctional puddle of bile.

Still, you will almost certainly return, probably many times, with a special affection for the City, born from your own personal, gritty experience. You'll be proud to say:

"New York is *my* town."

You'll carry around the street cred that attaches to anyone who's done a stretch in Manhattan. Tell outsiders you lived there, even for only a few years, and see what happens.

"You lived in New York City?! Wow!"

And this reaction makes sense because living in New York City *does* deliver life-changing experiences simply unavailable elsewhere. But the tuition at the University of NYC is dear, and it's collected day in and day out. So, living contentedly here also requires a periodic, sober review as to the currency of that good reason of yours and an understanding that there's a time to hold 'em and a time to fold 'em.

When I no longer had to be around Madison Square Garden every day and my corporate clients were indifferent as to where our offices were located, my wife pointedly asked what exactly was our continuing "good reason" for still maintaining offices and living in Manhattan, by then our home for nearly 40 years.

There was no good answer, because I was no longer drafting sufficiently off the City's resources. The give/get equation had gone awry. Even for a grizzled Manhattan chauvinist like me, time was up. The meter had expired. It was time to get out of Dodge.

P.S. Some people, however, choose to spend their entire lives in

Manhattan, even after retirement, feasting on its multitude of world-class entertainment, cultural, culinary, educational resources, to say nothing of its overall invigorating energy, happily contending with the relentless pace and not-so-controlled chaos of the place. Hey, whatever floats your boat. Everyone gets to define for themselves what may be *their* "good reason." There are no bad good reasons. Others, however, prefer to enjoy the place in measured doses now, and then retreat to the serenity of the country or the shore.

B. THE "FAIREST" OF THEM ALL

Among its many bests and firsts, New York City also turns out to be the fairest big city in the country, maybe the world.

Don't get me wrong. New Yorkers are not concerned about being "fair" or high-minded and are not even aware of this distinction. Not remotely. This version of fairness is the unintended consequence of New Yorkers' acute preoccupation with getting things done.

Here's what I mean:

Unlike Boston, Philly, Atlanta, Dallas, Houston, LA, or even Chicago, in Manhattan pedigree rarely matters. Particulars like where you're from, what college you went to, indeed *if* you went to college, and even what your last job was, don't count nearly as much here as elsewhere.

Now, you can't chop wood if you're not swinging an ax, so you do need access. You have to be in the room, and gaining access here is a major challenge, as it is everywhere. But in Manhattan, once you've been invited to that meeting, once you're sitting around that conference table, your pedigree isn't much help. Whether you're a jaded veteran or a wide-eyed newbie, New Yorkers will listen to what you have to say. And why not? They're already sitting in the room. Why not listen? Just maybe you'll be able to help advance their agenda. So initially they'll lean in and listen, and listen with equal focus to a Harvard MBA or a high school dropout.

YOU HAD YOUR CHANCE.

But maybe not for long. You must pick your shots, and be certain you know what you're talking about, because once you open your mouth you'll need to hold the audience and make a real contribution. Scrutiny will be immediate and withering, and if you miss the mark, the judgments will be swift and unforgiving. Eyes will roll and the window of opportunity will come down with the finality of a guillotine. And the invitation to the next meeting will never arrive.

But that's fair, no? That's a level playing field. You have no complaint. Ears were attuned. Eyeballs were fixated. The floor was yours. You had your chance, regardless of pedigree or credentials. That's all you can ask. In such an environment, fairness reigns.

4

THE ART OF NAMING

Selecting a name, whether for a child, a business, a book (indeed for *this* book), always surprises as to its difficulty.

Let's start with children. Were you to play by my rules, you'd do it like this:

First, no fudging when naming a kid after someone else. You get no credit for just matching first initials, the custom in some cultures. If you want to honor ol' Uncle Tobias, naming your kid Timothy or Thomas doesn't cut it. Truth be told, by doing so you've arguably insulted Uncle Tobias because what you're implying is that the name Tobias is unacceptable. Were you to formally name the child "Tobias," and then call him "Tommy," that passes the test, sort of, but isn't nearly as good as calling him Tobias in the first place.

Second, attend to euphony and rhythm between first and last names.

Middle names are less relevant to euphony because they're rarely spoken, whereas the first and last names become two parts of one whole and need to flow one to the other. Bill Goldstein is not notably euphonious, whereas Joshua Goldstein is.

CURIOUSLY, MIDDLE-NAMING IS OFTEN WHERE COUPLES GET STUCK.

Third, consider a first name that stands alone, immediately identifying its owner. You can do this by selecting a wacky name like "Breeze," a typically precious California selection I heard and harrumphed about recently. I think it best, though, to avoid hanging an off-the-wall handle on your child for the rest of their life. A simple yet distinct name like "Serena" does the trick nicely, often eliminating the need to use the last name at all.

That doesn't mean the middle name should be ignored or eliminated. It's still an opportunity to acknowledge someone, and curiously it's often where couples get stuck, as my wife and I did when naming our daughter.

We decided early on that her first name would honor her maternal grandmother. But for the middle name, we had three possibilities that we batted about endlessly. Finally, tired of our tedious indecision, we decided to try an old Irish naming ritual my wife had read about. She wrote the three contending names on separate pieces of paper, grabbed three identical candles, and with three-card monte dexterity put one name under each candle, lit the candles and declared:

"The name under the last candle burning will be it!"

"Brilliant," I responded with relief.

Of course, she'd picked mile-long candles, so all day and into the night we were checking the candles' progress. Ultimately, the candle above my late mother-in-law's maiden name inexplicably burned a full 90 minutes longer than the other two, a clear omen, and we confidently went with that name.

As it turns out, naming a business is no less challenging. When choosing a name for our sports marketing company my partner Ella Musolino (soon to become Ella Alber) and I originally considered the name "Good Sports." A smart-aleck friend of mine, wanting to highlight our well-known preoccupation with control, wrote a ditty using parts of our last names that went like this:

We'll use our "Muscle"
To get you "Gold"

We'll be "Good Sports"

If you do what you're told!

Ultimately, we settled on the duller, more businesslike option of "Sports Etcetera," with which my father, the Latin scholar, took issue:

> "You've improperly merged two words, 'Et' and 'Cetera'." Etcetera is not a word. You've forgotten your Latin, young man."

AND HOW HARD IS IT?

Thankfully, we didn't run into any other Latin aficionados along the way, and Sports Etcetera served our purposes quite nicely for 35-plus years.

P.S. One more thing about names. Why do so many immigrants anglicize their first names? Answer: They want to speed assimilation, but also — and this is the troubling part — because they assume, correctly, that Americans are too lazy to bother learning and using their real names. So Guadalupe becomes Gia, Bautista becomes Bob, Ignacio becomes Iggy, Leandro becomes Larry, and, indeed, Barack becomes Barry. Were you, however, to inquire as to their given name and ask that they spell and slowly pronounce it for you, and then you pronounce it yourself out loud until they confirm you've got it right, their reaction will absolutely fill you up. This simple measure of respect can make someone's day. They'll speak of it with their family and friends. And whenever you see them there'll be a spirit of friendship in the air.

And how hard is it? Surely we can all take the time to learn someone's name.

5

MEETING BILLIE JEAN KING

It's 1976. I was applying for a job with the New York franchise of World Team Tennis, unfortunately a largely unknown tennis format championed for decades by the great Billie Jean King. The last piece of the hiring process was an interview with the star herself. Instructed to come to her apartment at Lincoln Plaza at 7pm, I arrived in jacket and tie and was buzzed up, expecting to be ushered into a home office for a perfunctory five-minute feel-the-merchandise chat.

RELAX? HAVE SOME FUN? WAS HE NUTS?

After I lightly knocked, within seconds the door swung wide and there stood the one and only BJK, in tennis clothes, greeting me with this confounding question:

"Where's your stuff?"

"My stuff?? What stuff?"

"Your tennis gear, man. We're gonna have a hit. Didn't Larry tell you?"

"Ahh, not that I remember."

"No matter." Nothing ever unnerves Billie Jean, "You're about Larry's size."

AFTER 45 MINUTES SHE ABRUPTLY STOPPED.

Yelling to the back of the apartment to her then-husband Larry (not *that* Larry King, but a delightful fellow who was the president of the team and had interviewed me earlier in the day) to fix me up with tennis gear and send me down to the court, where she'd meet me.

Larry, a what-me-worry kind of guy and, as I would come to later appreciate, a notorious practical jokester, comes out from the back laughing his ass off and saying semi-apologetically:

"So sorry, guess I forgot to mention having a hit with Billie. Hey, just relax and have some fun."

Relax? Have some fun? Was he nuts? Completely discombobulated, frantically trying to figure out what the hell was going on, I struggled to maintain my composure. There's a tennis court in the building? Do they really care how I play? Aren't I being hired to sell tickets?

Synapses flying, I put on Larry's ill-fitting tennis shoes and shorts, while still wearing my black knee-length dress socks. No tennis shirt. Just took off my jacket and tie, loosened the collar of my shirt, took the racket Larry handed me and headed to the elevator, looking utterly ridiculous but resolved to follow Billie's lead and just "have a hit," figuring that this was a test about handling pressure.

Though I'm a pretty fair athlete, tennis was never my game. Pathetic serve. Embarrassing backhand. No court sense whatsoever.

As soon as I got on the court, Billie, already with a fistful of balls, started serving them up. It didn't take her long to realize that she had to keep it on my forehand if I was to have any chance of getting it back to her — which she did, still moving me all over the court, up and back, side to side, all the while bombarding me with these questions:

"How old are you? Are you married? How long? Kids? What does

27

your wife do? Do you exercise? What's your routine? For how long? Do you stretch first? For how long? Have you ever sold anything? What do you like about selling? What don't you like?"

Firing questions at me like a Gatling gun, while I struggled desperately to get the balls back across the net, or at least look good trying, she continued to grill me, bounding all over the court, questioning, laughing, judging.

SO PURE NON-DIVA.

"I understand you're a lawyer. Where'd you practice? Why'd you give it up? How are you gonna handle the players when they don't cooperate? How you gonna handle *me* when I don't cooperate?"

Finally, after 45 minutes, a long time for a little "hit," she abruptly stopped, came to the net, leapt over it from a standing stop as if she's just won Wimbledon, and declared:

"Larry likes you. I like you. If you're still interested, you're hired. We'd be lucky to have you."

It was so pure non-diva, so typically generous of spirit of Billie Jean, who in my judgment has only one peer with equivalent influence in the modern sports era: Muhammad Ali. And at the end of the day BJK's influence may well be greater — think Title IX, for openers.

6

A PRESIDENTIAL HISTORY LESSON

Born on July 4, 1872, and known by his middle name, John Calvin Coolidge Jr. was the 30th president of the United States.

History has largely forgotten Coolidge and when he is remembered it's not always flatteringly so. There were things he did, and things he didn't do, which some question. He was ultra-pro-business, favoring regulatory inaction which his detractors say hastened the Great Depression. Plus he was an isolationist, refusing to recognize the Soviet Union and not supporting the formation of the League of Nations.

Coolidge believed in small government and supporting the business community. His best-known quote, although actually a misquote, is:

"The business of America is business."

What he said was, "the chief business of the American people is business." Regardless, consider this:

Coolidge was a self-educated country lawyer who felt his job was to keep his clients *out* of court. He built his political career inch by inch, first as the mayor of Northampton, Massachusetts, where he lived with his family in a modest two-family home, then as lieutenant governor and eventually governor of the state.

COOLIDGE REFUSED.

His leadership during the Boston Police Strike of 1919 (exacerbated by the Spanish flu pandemic) made him a national figure, and in 1920 he was selected to run as Warren G. Harding's VP on the winning ticket.

On August 2, 1923, President Harding died suddenly from cardiac arrest and Coolidge succeeded him. He maintained most of Harding's policies, believing that Harding had been the one elected and his policies should not be altered. In 1924, Coolidge was nominated by the Republican party as its presidential candidate, and defeated the Democratic candidate, John W. Davis. Throughout the campaign he avoided conflict with his opponent, never even mentioning his name.

Coolidge connected well to the average middle-class citizen and was very popular. During his term the country experienced tremendous economic growth and the period came to be known as "The Roaring Twenties" (hard to fathom that we're now a full century down the road, just beginning a profoundly different version of our glorious Roaring Twenties).

In 1928 he decided *not* to seek reelection. Coolidge believed that if he were reelected he would be president for a total of 10 years and that that was too long to hold the reins of executive power. His Secretary of Commerce, Herbert Hoover, ran and won.

Coolidge was a quiet man, known as "Silent Cal." He knew that the words of a president had power and should be employed cautiously.

Because of the Great Depression during Hoover's presidency, many Republicans did not want Hoover to run in 1932 and tried to persuade Coolidge to come out of retirement and run again. He refused. Hoover was nominated and defeated in a landslide by the then-governor of New York, Franklin Delano Roosevelt.

These days, in 2020, there's much for our current president — and all politicians — to learn here, don't you think?

7

POCKETS

I don't know about you, but I won't wear a shirt, even a T-shirt, if it doesn't have a pocket. I mean, why in the world wouldn't you want a pocket? What, they ruin the "line" of your shirt? Seriously?

Pockets are a convenience. They're helpful. They're even more helpful with zippers, maybe not on shirts but certainly on jackets and sweatpants and shorts. Hell, I've got socks and belts and hats with zippered pockets. And if the pocket opening is vertical, as many are, the zipper should close by pulling down, much easier than pulling up. For me, function and comfort trump style and fashion. Hey, I like things that are easy on the eyes, too, but pockets do not disturb my aesthetic sensibilities.

P.S. Just learned that Robert Redford is partial to pockets too. Always liked the Sundance Kid.

8

GEORGE H.W. BUSH

Our company, Sports Etcetera, retained many five-star speakers over the years for corporate clients' big-time events. Sometimes these engagements produced unusual sidebars.

"OKAY, MAKE IT HAPPEN."

President George H.W. Bush was someone we engaged on more than one occasion. As a former president he automatically passed the will- the-guests-covet-a-photo-for-their-mantel test. Whether Democrat or Republican, a compelling or tedious speaker, all former POTUSes pass.

But not all former presidents are available. Jimmy Carter, even when robust, elected not to speak for hire. And following Warren Buffett's dictum that "price is what you pay; value is what you get," we never retained Bill Clinton because he's excruciatingly slow to commit, making his appearances maddening to promote, and therefore impossible to extract full value from. Plus, he's notoriously tardy, for me a no-no. Fact is, the roster of available speakers who pass the "mantel test" is always short (because sitting presidents, members of Congress, and governors are not permitted to give paid speeches), so former presidents are in high demand.

"YOU LOOK A LITTLE PEAKED."

During Bush 43's first term, we had a CEO client who insisted on having Bush 41 as a speaker at his annual big-ticket summer soiree. Having retained Bush 41 for a speech only a year previous, we reached out again, but were told that our California venue was out of the question. Forty-one intended to stay in Maine for the summer so he'd be there when 43 was able to get away to use it as the summer White House.

I reported back to my client, who predictably refused to take no for an answer and leaned on me hard to somehow make it happen.

"I know you've used him before and that you know his people. Press harder. I've already pumped up several of my more important guests telling them Bush is coming and you know how hard it is to get some of these people to attend. You must get H.W. for me."

Having anticipated the I-don't-accept-no-for-an-answer reaction, I was ready.

"The only way we get him is by changing the venue, which means forfeiting the $50k deposit we've already paid to the resort in California and moving to an ultra-convenient property for Bush. Turns out there's a fine resort in Ogunquit, Maine, not far from Kennebunkport. He could take his cigarette boat, which he loves to drive — fast — right from his own dock directly to the resort's dock. It could work."

"Okay, make it happen."

With a few calls — and a six-figure fee — the deal was sealed.

With former presidents any engagement is preceded by a site visit from the Secret Service to thoroughly scout out the venue. When we met with them to go over all the details, they confirmed that he would, indeed, be coming by boat and would need a place to freshen up before the breakfast speech.

"No problem," I said. "There's a gorgeous spa here, I'll block out a treatment room."

"One treatment room? No, no, you'll have to close the entire spa, for the whole morning."

"But there are a lot of treatment rooms," I gasped. "It'll cost a fortune to close the spa. Come on. Be reasonable."

"Our job does not include being reasonable, Mr. Goldstein. And we don't negotiate. Either you shut down the entire spa for the morning or he's not coming."

Realizing that these guys didn't care one iota about my problems, I bit my tongue and quickly acquiesced.

"All right, we'll do as you require. Anything else?"

"Yes. Your agenda indicates the speech is set for 10:30am, which means we'll arrive at about 10. He's a very punctual man. Often early. So be on the dock to receive him by 9:30. No later."

"I'll be there ... with bells on."

On the day of the event, I was waiting dockside at 9:15. About 9:25, I hear and then see Bush's sleek boat, *Fidelity* V, with him at the helm driving headlong at full tilt, his Secret Service detail holding on to the rails to steady themselves. By 9:30 he was off the boat, clearly animated by his high-speed trip.

"YOU LEAD AN INTERESTING LIFE. TELL ME A STORY."

"Mr. President, so very nice to see you again. Trust you had a nice ride here."

"Bracing. Very bracing. A glorious way to start the day."

"Excellent. Let me show you to the spa so you can freshen up."

"Spa? Freshen up? What are you talking about? I'm fine. I'm ready. Let's go do this thing."

"But sir, your people insisted that we buy out the entire spa for the whole morning so you could have a private, totally secure area to freshen up and rest a bit before the event."

"Nonsense. No need. They're always overly fussy. Sorry about that, but I'm good. Let's go."

"But, sir, we are not due until 10:30, nearly an hour from now. They're in a board meeting, and I can't just walk in with a former president. We'll have to wait. I'm terribly sorry."

I HEARD THE MUFFLED SOUND OF
MRS. BUSH SCOLDING HIM.

"Well, then, I guess we're going to get to know each other a little bit better, Bill. You okay? You look a little peaked."

"I'm okay, sir, just not used to killing time with former presidents."

"Well, you lead an interesting life. Tell me a story."

And don't you know, I just happened to have a pretty good story to share, and went on to explain that on the very day he and Mrs. Bush had their first child, Effie and Harold Goldstein had their last. Me.

"You're saying you were born on the very same day as George?"

"Yes, sir. That's right. Do you happen to remember what time the president was born? I think we were in the same time zone, too. I was born outside of Boston."

"We were in Connecticut. New Haven, to be precise. I'm afraid that's as much I remember. I don't recollect the time. But Barbara will. Give me your phone and let's call her."

Soon he had Mrs. Bush on the phone.

"Say, Barb, the organizer of this event tells me he was born the same day as George. What time was he born, honey?"

I heard the muffled sound of Mrs. Bush scolding him.

"I know, I know, I should have remembered. Okay, I'll tell him. 7:23 a.m., Eastern Standard Time. See you later, sweetie."

So that's how the day began. Ultimately, he delivered a delightful, anecdote-rich speech, which is exactly what we had requested.

And I learned that I was six minutes senior to the sitting president.

9

COCKTAIL HOUR TIPS

A. PACE

Cocktail receptions preceding big, fancy galas are frequently too long. Often much too long, where you stand around for an eternity waiting for the main event to begin. When the reception finally does end, you've eaten a dozen greasy stuffed mushrooms, had much too much to drink, and are dead on your feet desperate for a place to sit. Plus you've put a serious dent in your not-unlimited store of social repartee.

FIFTY MINUTES IS SUFFICIENT.

Any well-executed event requires pace. Overly long cocktail receptions torpedo pace, sucking the life out of a room. People are ready to leave before the dinner even starts. Better to keep it short. Indeed, the "cocktail hour" doesn't even have to last a full hour. Assuming people arrive together, 50 minutes is sufficient. An example of less being more.

B. COLOSSAL SHRIMP

Almost everyone loves to see shrimp at a cocktail reception, especially large shrimp. Indeed, the State Dining Room at the White House is renowned for its oversized shrimp.

Yes, normal shrimp are always well-received, too, but they don't deliver nearly the impact that big ones do. The bigger the better. People are unfailingly impressed with colossal shrimp, no matter the taste. Rubbery, flavorless... makes no difference. Size is all that matters. People will actually walk around at the reception, and even days later, exclaiming,

"Did you see the size of those shrimp?"

C. BARTENDERS

Never underestimate the number of bartenders needed at a function. Here, less is *not* more. With bartenders, less *is* less. Skimping on bartenders is a common mistake that ruins many events. People standing in line waiting for a drink is the kiss of death.

Having enough bartenders is also simple courtesy. All parts of an event are connected. As we learned in grade school, the neck bone's connected to the shoulder bone, etc. One mistake can sully the entire affair, while each wise decision builds in more quality. With sufficient bartenders, guests will consume more, become more exuberant, and are likely to have a better time, which, after all, is the whole idea, right?

PEOPLE ARE RIVETED, UTTERLY TRANSFIXED.

D. GIMMICKS

Cocktail receptions are significantly enlivened with the addition of clever, extra bits of entertainment, though it's an arrow in the quiver that often goes undeployed. People need more to do at these affairs. They need something to be distracted by, maybe something to interact with. Sometimes you see roving magicians or dancers or palm readers or mimes. All good. Anything whimsical and slightly offbeat works.

In a big space, my favorite gimmick is stilts. A guaranteed winner. People are riveted, utterly transfixed watching someone walk around on stilts. It's as if they're in the presence of Gulliver.

10

MY AMERICA'S CUP

The year is 1992. I'm busy negotiating and then implementing a major sponsorship deal for a Fortune 500 company in San Diego, the site of the quadrennial staging of the match race for the America's Cup — affectionately known as "Auld Mug" — the world's oldest international sporting trophy, dating back to 1851.

"I'VE SEEN YOU PULL A RABBIT OUT OF A HAT BEFORE."

My CEO client was a sailing fanatic who had retained our firm, Sports Etcetera, to secure a prime sponsorship for his company including — most importantly — the closest on-the-water viewing position possible.

The America Cup's organizers sold space on tricked-out viewing boats for fat cat corporate spenders like mine. But their viewing boats were large, clumsy crafts which were rightly kept quite a distance from the races — not remotely what my pampered CEO client had in mind.

"If I have to use binoculars, it doesn't work for me, Bill. I'll need to be inside the ropes."

"Inside the ropes?" restraining myself from telling him he'd lost his mind. "Only the competitors and the judges are inside the ropes. It's undoable."

"Nonsense. I've seen you pull a rabbit out of a hat many times before. That's why we pay you that fat monthly retainer. Work on it. I'll call you later."

Being a typically hyper-spoiled CEO accustomed to getting exactly *what* he wanted, *when* he wanted it, he didn't let up, staying on me like dots on dice every day to accomplish what was impossible.

Except ... I knew the TV commentator, whose small TV boat was the only other vessel allowed inside the roped-off race area. Because this was a growing client with a humongous event portfolio and we were working directly with the CEO, I decided to ask for a serious favor.

After bent-knee entreaties, the TV friend agreed to squeeze my client onto his boat, but not before this pointed admonition.

"What you're proposing is north of dumb. We'll be going 11 miles out into the ocean, where the surf is always roiling and unpredictable. Throws my little dinghy around like a kite. I'm certain this CEO of yours has exaggerated his experience, especially on a small rig like mine, which must dive in and out of the action at sharp angles for hours. If he comes, I'll greet him when he boards and then ignore him entirely. I'll have no food or drink or conversation for him all day. We'll be out there for 12 hours and if — make that when — he gets sick, it better not be inside my boat. Do this CEO of yours a favor and talk him out of this. It's a major mistake."

STUMBLING OFF THE BOAT, HE TURNED SLOWLY TOWARD ME.

Well, if I'd succeeded in talking him out of it, there'd be no story.

"Are you crazy? You hang the moon and then tell me to pass?" the CEO said, literally laughing in my face. "No bloody way. You've warned me. I'm good. Just tell me where and when."

46

Two days later, at 6am, he climbed aboard the modest 30-foot TV skiff with his little food cooler, greeting the three-man crew with:

"I'm very excited, haven't slept all night. Believe me, Bill gave me all the rules, in spades. I completely understand and will stay entirely out of your way. Don't even think about me. I'm not here."

Twelve long hours later, I met the boat at the dock. The TV commentator was knowingly shaking his head. My guy — whose face was a grim shade of green — staggered off the boat and, turning slowly toward me, faintly moaned in my ear:

"The worst fucking day of my life!"

As the saying goes, be careful what you wish for.

11

COMING IN OR GOING OUT?

At the beach, I like to set up shop close to the water's edge with an unobstructed view of the surf and where it's also always 10 degrees cooler. To avoid having to later uproot myself, I need to know whether the tide is coming in or going out, and when it will switch.

BUT YOU CAN'T TELL

BY LOOKING.

The idea, of course, is to not hastily plunk yourself down too close to the water and get swamped by an unanticipated incoming tide, nor set up too far from the water, where new arrivals could block a front row view by perching on real estate newly revealed by an ebbing tide.

So when I arrive at the beach it's immediately down to the water to inquire of earlier arrivals:

"Coming in, or going out?"

Typically I get a bewildered response:

"Coming in or going out???"

I clarify:

"The tide? Is it coming in, or is it going out?"

MORE NONSENSE.

Almost always, people are caught flatfooted.

"Gee, I don't really know," likely accompanied by an almost embarrassed look, as if thinking to themselves, "Hmmm, that's a good question."

Or sometimes I get,

"It looks like it's coming in."

But you can't tell by *looking*, unless you've been looking for a long time. Checking out whether the sand is wetter here or there and from that deducing whether the tide is coming in or going out is not reliable. Over short periods of time, waves are not perfectly progressive. Eyeballing just doesn't work.

Still, others respond,

"I think it's in between right now."

More nonsense. It's always either coming in, or going out. There's no "in between."

OCCASIONALLY, I GET REWARDED.

Often, even the preening lifeguards have no clue.

"I think high tide's soon," they might vaguely offer.

Soon? What exactly does "soon" mean? And aren't lifeguards getting paid to *know*, among other things, precisely when the tide changes? If they don't know that, what do they know?

And what's wrong with everyone else? Do they really want to scramble later to prevent their stuff from getting soaked? They know the ocean isn't frozen in place, right? But there they sit, oblivious, without a care.

Still, ever hopeful, I continue to go down to the water looking for guidance from a bright light. Occasionally I get rewarded by a kindred spirit who's actually paying attention. Always a sweet surprise.

12

BBQING

Where does it say that men must be good at, or even care about, BBQing? Everywhere, that's where. Here's what a Long Island magazine had to say recently:

> "Men of Long Island — feeling unmanly? Head out to the backyard and do what all self-respecting, manly American men do. Grill up some steaks. Be the Grill Master."

What a pathetic crock! If you must BBQ to secure your manhood, you're an irredeemable putz to start with.

BBQing is still cooking, right? There's lots of variables, making it maybe even more complicated than cooking on a stove. Gas vs. charcoal; high flame vs. low flame; meat vs. poultry vs. fish; marinades, glazes, rubs. Hell, even grilling a hotdog isn't simple. How exactly do you grill a cylindrical hot dog, evenly, on a flat surface without turning it, ever so slightly, a dozen times? Plus the paraphernalia ... spray bottles, basters, tongs, flippers, knives. Are we eating or operating?

And let's not forget the cleanup. Burned food, some disgustingly left over from last weekend's BBQ, or last month's ... maybe even last year's.

SORRY, PAL, NO SALE.

Look, I don't know how to cook or have the desire (or need) to learn, so why assume I know how to BBQ? Because it's camping-esque, which is supposed to be another natural male proclivity? Sorry, pal, no sale. Worse yet, why the presumption that men *like* to BBQ in the first place? What's to like? It's hot, smoky, greasy, and goes on interminably.

I'll shop; set the table; bartend; be a jolly host; even do the miserable cleanup. But become a "grill master?" Count me out.

And P.S., I can also do very nicely without camping.

13

A 10-SECOND TOASTER

Aha, I got your attention. Who wouldn't want their toast in 10 seconds?

Yes, toasters now come in sexy colors, with multiple, extrawide slots, peekaboo viewing windows, loading decks, "smart" technology with touchscreens, low thermal/steam heating elements, countdown clocks and chimes. But as to the time it takes to produce toast that's crispy on the outside and soft on the inside, speed is the critical variable, on which, astonishingly, there has been no improvement in my lifetime.

A company called Breville now includes a "Lift and Look" button that elevates the bread for a quick looksee, then slowly lowers it again if one cycle doesn't do the job, in which case there's also "A Bit More" button that lets you avoid committing to a full second round. All of which only serves to further reinforce the point that toasters are still too slow.

Even industrial toasters, the kind you see in hotels, where the toast goes around a heated loop and comes out the bottom, are slow as molasses, generally requiring a second go-round.

Think about the last time you were on a breakfast buffet line. If the proprietors were paying attention, they'd put the toaster at the *front* of the line so you could put in your bread, go get the rest of your food, circle back for your toast and sit down to enjoy a hot breakfast.

But no, toasters are always maddeningly placed at the *end* of the buffet. By the time you get there, because they're so bloody slow, there's always a line, people holding their food waiting to get at the toasters. At that point, you have four options ... all bad.

1. Wait your turn in the ubiquitous "toaster queue" while the rest of your food goes cold, eventually drop in your bread, and wait. Then maybe have to put it back down again, wait some more, collect your toast, and eventually sit down to eat a breakfast that is long past hot.

2. Wait your turn in the toaster queue, put in your bread, sit down, start to eat your incomplete breakfast while keeping an eye on the toaster, interrupt your meal to check on its progress, maybe more than once, and eventually claim your toast like it's a trophy.

3. Somehow wedge yourself into the toaster queue *before* plating the

rest of your food, wait to drop in your bread, abandon the toaster, get back in the regular line for the rest of your food, circle back for your toast, all while hoping the timing works out. A longshot, which will almost certainly result in a cold breakfast.

4. Or you can do what I do these days: privately curse both the pace and the placement of the toasters, skip the toast entirely, plate the rest of my food, and enjoy an immediate, hot, *toastless* breakfast.

SAYS EASY, DOES HARD.

And it isn't much better when you're at home. Toasters still take much too long, no matter the brand or model. Putting together a well-timed breakfast of eggs, bacon, and home fries with properly prepared hot toast — says easy, does hard.

Tell me. How is it that we can land a spacecraft on Mars, reproduce body parts (most recently a uterus, for heaven's sake), locate the most arcane information in a nanosecond on our smartphones, but can't figure out how to toast bread faster?

If there were 10-second toasters, they'd fly off the shelves.

14

RUDY GIULIANI IN HIS PRIME

Some of the pieces in Skip the Funeral were written a while ago, though thankfully none call out for an update ... except this one. As I ready this collection for publication in 2020, to ignore Giuliani's curious, often bewildering role as the President's personal lawyer/foreign emissary would be as if to serve this up in a time capsule, which is not the intent. Suffice it to say, therefore, that by finagling his way into Trump's orbit, Giuliani has certainly refashioned his place in history. I'll leave it at that.

It's the summer of 2007. Donald Trump is simply a tediously self-promoting real estate developer. Rudy Guiliani — owing to his post-9/11 notoriety and name recognition as "America's Mayor" — is reveling in his fame, and has become the early frontrunner for the 2008 Republican presidential nomination. His candidacy would later crater in the swamps of Florida, with John McCain ultimately winning the nomination, only to himself get swamped by Barack Obama in the general. But in August 2007 Rudy was riding high, leading in both the national polls and fundraising.

We were shopping for a high-profile keynote speaker for a major corporate confab we executed annually. Needing someone with automatic drawing power, and because public officeholders are not permitted to speak for hire, the pool of available top-tier "talent" was quite thin. Thankfully, our client wanted Rudy. He was out of office and hence available, and getting major media attention. For that singular moment in time, he was the hottest speaker on the circuit, commanding a high fee, private jet, and all manner of additional perks.

We retained him for a speech at the Le Manoir Richelieu, a gorgeous, historic property in La Malbaie, Quebec, sited on a cliff overlooking the mighty St. Lawrence River about 90 miles northeast of Quebec City. A chateauesque French castle with its grand boardwalk stretching broadly above the river, the hotel is spectacular, albeit inconveniently located.

Because Giuliani was in such high demand, his agent was able to impose all sorts of ego-driven demands: a fat six-figure fee, the hotel's Presidential Suite, three additional rooms for his handlers, plus a large twin-engine private jet.

When retaining speakers, if our target was hot and their demands within shouting distance of being reasonable, we went along, but we insisted on a substantial increase in the speaker's responsibilities, well beyond what was commonly required. We'd pay, but Giuliani's normal routine of arriving an hour before a speech, talking for 50 minutes, answering a few questions, spending 20 minutes taking photos and then splitting would not remotely suffice.

"YOU'RE TELLING ME THAT MISERABLE RIDE WAS AVOIDABLE?"

He'd have to arrive at the hotel at least six hours before the speech; autograph copies of his memoir for each guest; participate in a full photo session during a 60-minute cocktail reception preceding the speech; make his speech; take questions for 30 minutes; stay for dinner sitting at the CEO's table; and be pulled around the room to touch up various other VIPs. These requirements were nonnegotiable and all the major speaking agencies knew it. We'd run an impeccably buttoned-up event, take good care of their client, pay full freight complete with all the trimmings, and not whine about it. But we required a lot for our money, or we would hire someone else.

About a week after the deal with Rudy had been finalized, I realized that his demand for a large twin-engine jet would make it impossible for him to take advantage of the small private airport located conveniently near the hotel. Instead, he'd have to fly into Quebec City and be driven to the Chateau, an unpleasant 90 miles with mountainous switchbacks the entire way. A tortuous drive that I had made myself on a site visit months earlier. I tried to explain the problem to his agent, whom I knew well.

"We'll charter the bigger plane if you insist, but it'll mean he must land at Jean Lesage International Airport, Quebec's primary airport. I can tell you from firsthand experience the drive from Jean Lesage to the hotel is perfect misery. If we go with a smaller plane, he can land five minutes from the hotel. Believe me, that's the better plan."

"We definitely need the bigger plane, Bill. I'm not even going to take your suggestion to him. He's really feeling his oats these days and won't even listen. He'll just go apeshit."

This explains, in one sentence, why despite being a lawyer I never seriously considered becoming an agent for athletes or celebrities. Too much ego-driven maintenance. Too many decisions made for the wrong reason.

"As you please, but if he arrives at the hotel in a foul mood, bitching about the horrendous drive, this conversation will be repeated to him. This is a bad call."

"It's on me, Bill. Please just make the arrangements. I'll deal with Rudy."

And so it went. On the appointed day, when I greeted Giuliani upon his arrival at the hotel, he was, just as I had feared, north of agitated.

"What an atrocious trip up here. Why didn't you do this in Quebec City, for God's sake."

"Mr. Mayor, I told your agent to let me charter a smaller plane so you could land minutes away at the local private airport. But he was afraid of your reaction and rejected my counsel."

"What a witless pussy. You're telling me that miserable ride was avoidable? Unfuckingbelievable!"

After completion of the meal and all his responsibilities, Rudy's posse was hovering outside the dining room waiting with his prized humidor, filled with the priciest, most rarefied cigars on the planet. Soon they set up shop for a late-night puff-fest on the boardwalk outside the hotel overlooking the St. Lawrence.

I was about to call it a night when my client grabbed me, explaining that one of his most important guests had failed to get Giuliani to autograph their book and asked me to find Rudy and get the book signed.

Dutifully, though reluctantly, I marched out to the boardwalk, found

Rudy chomping on a fat cigar, asked him for "one last favor," and was greeted with this:

"Man, you don't quit, do you?"

I WAS AS SICK AS I'D BEEN IN YEARS.

I placed my hands together in prayerful pose.

"Okay, okay, I'll sign it, but first, sit down and try this beauty," he said, handing me the longest cigar I'd ever seen.

"Ahh, sorry, Mayor, I don't smoke. Disagrees with me."

"Goldstein, I've done more stuff at this gig for you than I've ever done for anyone. Much more. Got here way early. Cocktail reception. Photos. Book signing. Speech. Long Q&A. Dinner with your CEO, interrupted three times by you hauling me all over the room to table-hop. Plus that nauseating ride up here, which must be repeated in the morning. And now this extra bit. You want that book signed? Sit down and light up. It'll do you good. These are phenomenal cigars. Best in the world. Shouldn't make you sick. Sit down. Take a load off, for Christ's sake."

Needing the book signed, I was stuck, sat down as instructed, and lit up while he inquired.

"I'll probably never pass this way again. Tell us what you've come to know about this place, Bill."

So I held forth a bit about what I'd learned about the St. Lawrence Seaway and its intricate system of locks, canals, and channels designed to bypass rapids and dams, allowing oceangoing vessels to travel from the Atlantic Ocean as far inland as Duluth, Minnesota. The locals lovingly referred to the Seaway as Highway H_2O. After about 30 minutes of this, which Rudy seemed especially fascinated by, and with a respectable amount of accumulated ash, I handed him the book, got his John Hancock, wished him safe travel, and took my leave.

Fifteen minutes later, back in my room at last, I was as sick as I'd been in years, owing to that pricey stogie.

15

HUNTERS

As in days of old, modern men are hunters too; they just don't know it.

Here's what I mean.

Most men regularly get sent out by their significant other with a "To Do" list. Get this. Get that. Go here. Go there.

"HOW'S THE HUNTING GOING?"

From then on, hombres, we're hunters, not for an 800-pound moose but for an impossible-to-find Sicilian olive oil or a specialty no-fat Greek yogurt or some rarefied lotion from a boutique apothecary.

And if you come home empty handed, you're a fuckup!

"This is yogurt, but not Greek, and it's 1%, not no-fat. These crackers are neither low-sodium nor whole-wheat. And where's the dry cleaning? I gave you a list, right?"

So here are a few tips for fellow hunters.

When you arrive at a supermarket, go immediately to customer service to get the correct aisle for every item on your list, rather than bumbling around from aisle to aisle, cluelessly, like a nomad in the desert. Take advantage of one of the few instances — shopping — when men get sympathy, topped only by when we're caring for a baby. The world stops in its tracks to help inept-looking fathers contend with an infant. Shopping with a baby in tow is the ultimate sympathy play.

It also helps to be self-depreciating. Check your pride at the door.

"Could you help this struggling husband?" never fails.

Sometimes I'm able to get the customer service attendant to walk me directly to the sought-after items, a huge timesaver which also avoids missing something right under my nose, which I manage to do with stunning frequency.

And when I see other men in the same boat, or should I say the same wilderness, stumbling around aimlessly, desperate to cross items off *their* lists, occasionally I reach out with brotherly empathy.

"How's the hunting going?"

IT ALWAYS TRIGGERS A WIDE SMILE.

And then I give them this same rap and it always triggers a wide smile and new appreciation for their role.

"Yeah, that's right, goddamn it. I'm a freaking hunter!"

16

FRUIT

A really sweet piece of fruit can be wonderfully satisfying. For me, as nice as an enticing zillion-calorie dessert.

The problem is *finding* a really sweet piece of fruit. Mission Impossible.

With fruit, one bite tells the story. If that first bite's no good, there's no point bothering with the rest. It's not getting any better.

With most fruits there's a wide range between terrific and terrible. You never know what you're going to get. Bananas are the exception. They're predictable, but when's the last time you heard someone say,

"What a terrific banana I just had."

And a banana is no substitute for a bowl of ice cream. An exquisitely sweet Georgia peach just might be. But go find one. Most peaches we get are mealy and tasteless. Fact is, you'd be smart to skip peaches altogether and go with nectarines, which may be the most reliably sweet fruit of all.

BUT THIS IS UNRELIABLE AND OBNOXIOUS

— AND WORSE.

Plums? Ha! A decent plum is even harder to find than a decent peach. They're almost always hard, flavorless, and yellow on the inside. I want a plum that's ruby red on the *inside*. Don't get fooled by the "red plum" sticker either, which refers to only the *exterior* color, and who cares about that? When they're right, plums are my favorite, my holy grail of fruit, though I don't expect to be enjoying one anytime soon.

Pears are complicated. For some reason, apart from apples, super-markets often offer a wider variety of pears than any other fruit — Bartlett, Seckel, D'Anjou, Comice and sometimes those massive Asian pears nestled in their own pretentious Styrofoam cradle. Lots to choose from, but it's hard to find one that's softer than a baseball. Mostly it's one bite and straight to the trash, if you can get your teeth into it at all.

I suppose it's possible to improve your chances by squeezing or smelling fruit before you buy it and somehow divining its worthiness. But what gives someone the right to maul a piece of fruit, then toss it back in the pile for the next person to take home, covered with their germs? This is not only unreliable and obnoxious but, worse, potentially deadly, as we adapt to the era of coronavirus.

And if you choose to buy fruit before it's ripe and don't pay close attention to it every day, it's apt to ripen too much before you remember to eat it. When I buy fruit, I'd like it to be ready to eat. Soon. Today. Tomorrow for sure. Putting it aside and patiently calibrating its ripeness for days? Isn't that the vendor's job? If it's not ready to eat, or almost ready, what's it doing in the bin?

17

VICE-PRESIDENT AL GORE

At all bigtime corporate events featuring major speakers, it's *de rigueur* for each guest to take a photo with the speaker. This is especially so if the speaker passes the mantel test. That is, the speaker is famous enough for people to wish to display the photo on their fireplace mantel.

If the host corporation's logo is somehow also captured in the photo, well, that's the state of the art. This can sometimes be accomplished by staging the shoot in front of a corporate banner, but with the varying heights of the subjects, the relative position of the banner, and the unreliability of the photographer, the host's logo doesn't always make it into the picture. The bulletproof approach is to have the speaker wear a shirt or sport jacket bearing the host's logo, which they'll do *if* it's included in the contract, which with us was a given.

Unlike some former vice presidents who don't pass the mantel test — Dan Quayle, and dare I say, perhaps Mike Pence down the road — Al

Gore in the year 2000, having just left office with the prospect of running for president himself, was a hot political property and passed the mantel test.

We retained him to give a speech at a resort in the Caribbean. Our deal with his agent prominently included the he-must-wear-the-logoed-polo-shirt-we-provide clause as a "material" provision, legalese for saying it's central to the deal.

AN UNHAPPY AL GORE WOULD DESTROY THE EVENT.

The event was a morning speech for which Gore had arrived the previous evening. We had a logoed polo shirt waiting in his suite with a note reminding him to wear it the following morning, and if the size was not right, we had others.

About 9pm, I called his suite to make sure he was comfortable and to suggest that he order room service for breakfast and that I would be at his door at 10am sharp to escort him to the meeting room.

"Fine," he said, "But what's with this shirt you've left for me? I'm here to deliver a speech, not endorse your client."

"Mr. Vice President, we're not asking for an endorsement. Just photos with you in the shirt. Nothing more."

"Sorry, can't do it."

"Sir, the last thing I wish to be is argumentative, but wearing the logoed shirt is a material provision in our Agreement. For me it's a must-have. I'd be happy to show you the contract."

"No need to see the contract. I believe you. But I consider this request an implied endorsement, which I never agreed to make. I'm just not comfortable wearing the shirt. I hope you understand."

At this point, I had two choices. Either push back further, maybe insist on getting his agent on the phone and try to enforce the deal. Or, to ensure that Gore was a happy camper, forget the silly shirt and rely on a logoed banner being properly hung behind the photo location. An unhappy Al Gore, with or without the shirt, would destroy the event. The choice was an easy one.

"I do understand, Mr. Vice President. The CEO will not be happy, but they never are. I know I can rely upon you to pay special attention to him and his wife."

"Absolutely. Just point me in the right direction. You won't be disappointed. I appreciate your understanding on this, Bill. And please, call me Al."

From then on, the wind was at my back. Gore was very solid and left to a standing O. We also managed to salvage the photo shoot, despite the absence of the logoed polo shirt, which in jest I told Gore to keep as a memento.

HEY, FAIR'S FAIR.

Later that week, however, I negotiated a $10,000 reduction in Gore's fee, owing to the breach of the shirt provision. My guess is that Gore got his full net, with the agency taking a major haircut on its commission. Hey, fair's fair; a deal's a deal.

18

ARENA NOISE

Growing up in Boston as a sports fanatic, I just about lived in the old Boston "Gahden" and at Fenway "Pahk."

As a promoter, I have staged over 1000 events. Safe to say, arenas, ballparks, and concert halls are all familiar territory to me, both as a fan and as a professional. But these days you'd have to horsewhip me to attend any public sporting event in which I wasn't directly involved. Why? Because the gratuitous noise in arenas has by now gone way beyond the pale.

In days gone by, people continuously exchanged banter while watching a live event. The repartee was as much a part of the experience as the event itself. Not so today.

Programmed music is so ear splittingly loud, tasteless, and coming at you without letup that, remarkably, talking is impossible.

You have to yell to be heard. Even — make that especially — during timeouts or between quarters or halves, there is no letup and the mindless cacophony actually *increases*.

SUCH CIVILIZED MOMENTS ARE LONG GONE.

It used to be that these natural breaks were pleasant interludes of relative quiet which patrons looked forward to. A time when you could catch your breath and have an extended exchange with your neighbor. Today, such civilized moments are long gone.

Furthermore, any authentic fan doesn't need to be harangued by a fifty million dollar scoreboard. They don't want to be told when to cheer, much less how. All the deafening prompts and banal group remonstrations are off putting in the extreme.

But by embedding all this discordance, the promoters are unwittingly admitting that the event itself is *insufficient*. In effect they're saying:

"Without including this shrill, shameless racket the event could not hold the audience's attention."

Perhaps they're right. Scientists tell us that in 2020 the average person has an eight-second attention span, less than a goldfish, which apparently can concentrate for nine seconds. So maybe without catering to the lowest common denominator and imposing this ceaseless, low-rent group cheerleading imperative, big crowds wouldn't come out today.

But for me, it's too much. To think that in order to attract today's fan you must subvert the fundamental spectator experience is way messed up. By baking in all the needless noise and thus making normal, contemporaneous conversation impossible, the baby has been thrown out with the bathwater.* It's FUBAR.**

*According to one online account, in medieval times families bathed in their scarce bathwater by age, elders first. By the time a baby got its turn, the water was so murky that the baby was in danger of being dumped out unseen, though I expect this fascinating bit of purported etymology is an old wives' tale.

**Google FUBAR if you're unfamiliar with this apropos acronym originated by our overwrought soldiers in WWII.

19

JAMES CARVILLE & MARY MATALIN

You know these two. James is the rabid Democratic operative. Mary, calmer and more polished, is the just as all-in Republican operative. Our company retained them to speak in tandem at a client's event.

WHEN I SAW HIM LATER, JAMES WAS STILL FUMING.

James and Mary agree on nothing of substance politically and yet seemingly have been happily married for many years. It's hard to process how two people could virulently disagree on everything political and still reside under the same roof.

After introducing them to the audience, I sat back and waited for the fireworks. They ham-and-egged it for an hour or so, poking spirited fun at each other and their respective political patrons, telling semi-out-of-school stories about the most compelling public figures of our time.

Great fun and exactly why we engaged them.

Then came the Q&A, and after a few benign, forgettable questions, one guy rose and served up the one that was on everyone's mind but which nobody else had had the stones to ask.

> "So tell me," he said, in a needlessly sarcastic manner, "Are you two cynical about politics or marriage? Which is it?"

IT'S NO ACT.

Carville's face went beet red. He looked over at me, standing in the wings, as if to say:

> "You let this classless toad in?"

Still, he gathered himself, and went on to offer a vanilla response saying that they're able to compartmentalize. When I saw him later he was still fuming.

> "Can you believe that guy? What a rude prick!"

I thought he had missed the point.

> "The guy could have been more tactful, but how you two stay married while fighting hammer and tong about all the things you hold dear politically is an enigma to every audience you speak before. And don't tell me it's none of their business. It's who you are as a public couple. It's your calling card. It's why we retained you both. It's what makes you compelling. Not only should you be *willing* to talk about it, you should anticipate the question and be *proud* to answer it."

Truth is, the answer to the guy's question is that they are cynical about neither marriage nor politics. Their uncommon ability to live harmoniously together, to love each other, and still vehemently disagree about so many important issues may well astound the rest of us.

But it's no act. They are the real deal.

20

PHARMACISTS

Why are pharmacists so often barricaded behind elevated, impenetrable, plexiglass shields through which they seem to hear only what they want to hear?

Yes, I know that the drugs must be safely secured, but that doesn't mean the pharmacists must hide out in a pharmaceutical bunker.

WHAT IF, HEAVEN FORBID, CUSTOMERS WANT TO TALK FACE TO FACE?

What if someone has a sensitive health concern and doesn't want it relayed to the pharmacist by a clerk? What if, heaven forbid, they want to talk face to face? Very often even to talk discreetly the pharmacists still won't come down from their lofty perch. In such a circumstance the customer can either not pursue their question or raise their voice and lob a private health concern up over the pharmacist's off-putting barrier for all the world to hear.

Why the lack of sensitivity? Why the isolation?

What are they, monks?

21

CELL PHONES

Our cellphones have become what guns must have been like in the Old West. Indispensable. We don't go anywhere without them. If we lose them, we feel helpless and vulnerable until we "rearm" ourselves.

OUR PHONES ARE OUR GUNS.

We even keep them in holsters, except at meals, when we plant them on the table ready to grab at a moment's notice.

Our phones are our guns. Our only can't-do-without item.

On a related question, why is it okay to talk to someone next to you on a public conveyance, but not okay to talk on a public conveyance to someone if they're on the other end of your cell phone?

In both instances, the only relevant issue is volume, not proximity. If you don't talk too loud, what's the problem?

YOU'D PROBABLY GET ARRESTED.

And while we're at it. Whatever happened to whispering in libraries, which used to be required? Today, whispering in libraries isn't even encouraged. Even the librarians talk at street volume. What about not disturbing those around you trying to concentrate? A forgotten protocol, I guess, although were you to talk in a library at normal volume on a cellphone you'd probably get arrested.

22

GIFT CERTIFICATES

I hate 'em. To me, they're not "gifts." They're headaches.

Say someone gives you a gift certificate, perhaps to a clothing store. If you were to immediately run down to that store and spend *precisely* the value of the certificate, well, then everything would be jake.

But that's not what happens.

Often people tuck away a gift certificate someplace "safe" for later use. Then, if they're anything like me, they forget where they put it or, indeed, forget about it altogether. In time, it goes missing.

Or it expires. And why exactly should a gift certificate expire? Has the money it was bought with expired?

If the gift certificate isn't lost, doesn't expire, and is actually used, often it's only partially used, in which case the merchant inevitably gives you yet *another* gift certificate for the unconsumed balance, because, of course, they'd never consider giving you the balance back in cash. But why not? They were paid in full long ago, weren't they?

RUBBISH.

YOU WERE JUST LAZY.

Or even worse, you bring your gift certificate into the store and end up spending *more* than its value. Now the "gift" has *cost* you money.

Businesses love gift certificates. In 2019, over $1 billion in gift certificates went unredeemed in the U.S. — a huge windfall for merchants. Even those that are eventually used provide the merchant with an interest-free loan for what could be years. Further, when people buy gift cards they are unwittingly agreeing to promote the store whose gift cards can't be used elsewhere and assure the retailer that the recipient will either come in to redeem the card and perhaps spend beyond its limit, or not use it at all, both wins for the merchant.

And never mind the giver's self-serving declaration:

"I wanted to make sure you got something you wanted."

Rubbish. You were just lazy.

You want to give someone a proper gift? Do it the right way. Spend some time thinking about, and then buying something they might like. If you're unable or unwilling to do that, hey, that's okay. Just admit it and give money. We know that won't expire or go to waste.

23

WORDS AND PHRASES

A. "HECK"

I wince whenever I hear someone use the word "heck," as in:

"What the heck."

Or

"You scared the heck outta me."

Or as I heard Rachel Maddow declare recently when describing a raucous Trump rally,

"Several varieties of heck broke out."

Is she kidding? Could there be a more ungainly turn of phrase? Is there a more awkward word in the English language?

You can actually *feel* the awkwardness when people use "heck." They know how stilted and inauthentic they sound. Still, despite their discomfort they use it anyway, too timid and dare I say cowardly, even in 2020, to say what they really want to say and crank out:

THERE, YOU HEAR HOW FALSE AND EMPTY IT SOUNDS?

"You scared the crap outta me."

Or,

"What the hell."

Never mind, and heavens to Betsy,

"What the fuck."

Still, let's be quick to note that those who gratuitously drop F-bombs every other word, whether to shock, establish street cred or whatever, well, they're just boring and vulgar. Period.

With profanity, less is more. As Stephen King instructs, the only relevant question "is not whether language is sacred or profane, but rather, how true it rings on the page or in the ear." If profanity is used selectively, when it's inescapably the best choice, by a self-assured person with command of the language who knows how to be effectively profane (and not everyone does), profanity becomes an extra option in the wordsmith's toolbox, an enrichment of the language, even poetry, and is a heck of a way to enliven your vocabulary.

There, you hear how false and empty it sounds? I can barely get it out, even in ridicule.

B. "BACK IN THE DAY"

You often hear people of all ages, some even in their 20s, describing something that happened "back in the day."

Back in what day? Two years ago? Five years ago? Ten years ago?

Sorry. To borrow from Bill Maher, we need a new rule: You don't get to use "back in the day" unless you're referring to something that happened decades ago. Over and out.

C. "TO BE HONEST"

Lots of people use "to be honest" or one of its derivatives ("to tell you the truth" or "in all honesty") almost reflexively, in an effort to underscore their sincerity. A sort of verbal tic. Occasionally it's useful, softening a message, making it easier to tell someone something you know they don't want to hear. I'm told its use is popular with some millennials, who often even abbreviate it with "tbh." Nevertheless, it's a bad habit.

DOES THAT MEAN THEY AREN'T TELLING THE TRUTH?

For openers, when we hear it, we likely have a moment of confusion, even dread, not knowing what's coming next. The uncertainty is unsettling. Sentences that start with "to be honest" do not generally end well.

More importantly, telling someone you're about to be honest doesn't *make* you honest, and more to the point, being honest should not require an announcement.

Abe Lincoln loved riddles. One of his favorites underscores the point.

Question: If you call a tail a leg, how many legs does a dog have?

Answer: Four. Calling a tail a leg doesn't make it a leg.

To me, the use of these phrases suggests the speaker is nervous about what they're about to say and that, indeed, it may be *less*, not more, trustworthy. The listener is not reassured, but rather likely left with heightened doubt. And if a person who regularly uses these vacuous phrases should elect on occasion to *not* use them, does that mean that on those occasions they *aren't* telling the truth?

Bottom line: These phrases are almost always disingenuous. Naturally you want people to believe you're telling the truth. But this is accomplished by building a reputation for veracity, not by relying upon self-serving claptrap which creates a contrary impression.

D. "RESONATE"

Sometimes the world latches on to a word and just won't let go. The favored word gets picked up by everyone and used incessantly.

These days, Fall of 2020, that word is "resonate," which we all hear with nauseating frequency, as if it makes the user sound erudite and worldly.

It doesn't. It makes them sound tiresome and unoriginal.

For openers, the term "resonance" comes from physics: the tendency of an object to vibrate at a given frequency, and specifically when one object naturally vibrates at the natural frequency of a second object. Until recently, it was usually employed with sound, often music, since what we hear is caused by "resonant" vibrations.

IT'S BECOME A TOTAL BANALITY.

But now it's everywhere. You can't go through a single day without hearing it, several times, especially by the talking heads on TV. What did we use before "resonate" became so fashionable? I'm not sure. And that's the problem. Spot-on synonyms don't come immediately to mind.

Still, the word "resonate" has by now been squeezed bone-dry. There's nothing left. So please, *no mas*. Stop hauling into service this terribly tired word which has by now been sapped of all its power. Indeed, sapped of its resonance.

While we're at it, let's also confine to the same linguistic dust bin *artisanal* and *conflate* and *narrative* and *curate*. All nearly as overused and vapid as *resonate.*

And most especially, we must muzzle the fatiguing, tedious, pretentious use of "existential," which is so worn out that it's become a total banality. Every problem is not an "existential" crisis.

Curiously, these days, with this massive coronavirus mess, there's finally an appropriate *narrative* with which to righteously employ two of these irritating words, to wit: "This pandemic is an existential threat which resonates with everyone." Since the last pandemic was in 1918, I hope it'll be another hundred years before they're both heard together again.

24

GORE VIDAL

Taking a question after a dinner speech at one of our client shindigs, Gore Vidal, the public intellectual and novelist known for his wit and patrician style, was asked a tantalizing question.

Q: "What do you think would have happened in 1963 if Khrushchev, not Kennedy, had been assassinated?"

Vidal: "With history, one can never tell, but I think it's safe to say that Aristotle Onassis would not have married Mrs. Khrushchev." *

The best improvised one-liner I've ever heard.

*For those who may not remember Nina Khrushchev, let's just say that she, like her husband, Nikita, embodied the stout Russian peasant look.

25

HENRY KISSINGER

From time to time it's been my pleasure to host world-class business and political leaders when they attended our events. On one such occasion the special guests were Henry Kissinger and his statuesque wife, Nancy, who had come to the finals of our Virginia Slims Women's Tennis Championships at Madison Square Garden.

A TRUE FAN.

I had done a little research and knew that ever since fleeing Germany and the Nazis, in 1938, Kissinger had closely followed his hometown's soccer club, SpVgg Greuther Fürth. Over cocktails in Suite 200 — the ultra-VIP hospitality venue at the Garden — I asked him about his affinity for his hometown team.

"My experiences in Germany were not very positive, including simple pleasures like rooting for my hometown team. When the Nazis came in it was a risky proposition for Jews to go to a crowded place like a soccer stadium. We'd get beaten up. Irrationally, I went anyway. I still follow the team. I'm not sure why I still care, but I do."

A true fan. Then pivoting to U.S. soccer, he inquired,

"Do you think that soccer will ever really make it here? What's the view of the sports community? What do you think?"

"Well," I began slowly, weighing whether to be entirely candid, then deciding, why not? "No. I'm afraid I don't believe the future is especially bright for U.S. soccer. Too subtle, too nuanced for Americans. It's all passing. Not enough shooting, never mind enough scoring for the U.S. audience. Sort of like baseball for Europeans. Too slow. Too many inexplicable rules."

"I understand. Although I must say I love the Yankees, so I don't fit your profile. But what you say makes sense to me."

Then, curious about the building and what went on in the bowels of Madison Square Garden, he asked if I'd give them an insider's tour. I was happy to oblige.

Mid-tour, after hearing me labor trying to explain something simple to a subordinate who had tracked me down and mindlessly interrupted with a triviality, Kissinger put his hand on my shoulder, leaned toward me, whispering in my ear:

> "You can *explain* things to people, Bill, but you cannot *understand* for them."

First-rate advice.

26

STUBBLE & TOUSLED HAIR

I'm watching TV the other day and there's Ben Affleck opining as if an expert on issues of considerable import with his hair all askew and sporting heavy stubble. So what, Ben, you didn't have time to take a shave or comb your mop?

WHAT FEEBLE NONSENSE.

Or no, I get it, tousled hair and stubble are now both required among the Hollywood woke.

Come on. If you want to be taken seriously and hold forth on global issues, then grow up, clean up, and present yourself like an adult.

Of course, Affleck has plenty of company. Jeremy Piven, who played the Hollywood agent in HBO's *Entourage* series, is an equally prime culprit.

And Liev Schreiber, the lead stud in the Showtime hit *Ray Donovan*, is yet another who has perfected the stubble look morning, noon, and night. And of course their ancestor was *Miami Vice*'s Don Johnson.

What, these guys never shave? Or when they do, they always leave stubble so they're never, ever clean-shaven? Maybe they're using one of these new electric razors made to deliver what Norelco defines as "a flawlessly unkempt 5-o'clock shadow look." What feeble nonsense.

Then there's Kevin Bacon, with his juvenile tousled hair. The guy's over 60 years old and chooses to present himself like a nervous teenager.

And it's not just movie stars. It's everyone. It's everywhere. From Melrose Avenue to Wall Street, male models in print, television, billboard and internet advertisements all sport the compulsory stubble *cum* tousled hair combo, often with a few tattoos to enhance their "street" appearance.

Every wannabe pretty boy has bought into this happy horseshit believing somehow that if they maintain a stubbled mug and tousled coiffure they'll look sexier, tougher, hipper.

Worse still, they actually want us to believe that their look is not deliberate. That it's happenstance. That they're just so incredibly casual and loosey-goosey that they scarcely recall whether they've shaved or combed their hair at all. It's the male equivalent of women laboriously trying to achieve the no-makeup look while wearing tons of it.

The desired effect in both cases is a confident insouciance. The intended message: they didn't prepare or do anything special before going out in the world. It's the effortless, indifferent look, ironically achieved after painstaking effort.

THIS "LOOK" HAS BECOME A MEASURE OF CONFORMITY.

Indifferent? Ha! Every hair on their sorry heads has a half pound of goo on it and the length of their stubble has been calibrated within a millimeter. Their look is not a fluke or accidental. They haven't just emerged from an all-night poker game, or a long red-eye from the Coast. No. It's deliberate and cultivated — and lame.

And when older guys with graying stubble fall prey, it looks especially pathetic. They don't look insouciant or *au courant*, they look disheveled and old (think Harvey Weinstein). Worse, the popularity and misperception of the stubble look provide cover for seniors to be unkempt and sloppy, encouraging an ill-advised I-don't-give-a-damn attitude about their overall appearance. Not good.

When younger guys do it — because it's become so commonplace — they also don't appear hip, they just look like everyone else. Ironically, it has become a measure of *conformity*, not individuality.

Black T-shirt. Check.

Stubble. Check.

Tousled hair. Check.

Yawn. Double-check.

27

POLS AND BIG FAMILIES

My father had a rule about politicians. If they had more than four kids, he wouldn't vote for them, unless they were rich.

"HE CAN'T POSSIBLY SUPPORT HIS FAMILY."

His thinking: if a politician has lots of children, he can be bought (regrettably, there were few women politicians at the time).

> "He can't possibly support his family on his modest salary without being vulnerable to corruption."

My father would have loved Michael Bloomberg. A Boston boy (yep, the three-term former mayor of NYC is from Medford, Massachusetts). Just two kids. And so rich as to be presumptively incorruptible.

28

ISSUES AT RESTAURANTS

In the fall of 2020, with the coronavirus pandemic still heavily influencing our lives, it'll be awhile before people start eating in restaurants regularly again. But when things open up — assuming the quality of the food passes muster — the most important consideration for me when selecting a restaurant will remain comfort. The physical space has to be commodious, especially now.

WHAT A CROCK!

Hence the first restaurants eliminated from consideration are those with long banquettes against each wall accompanied by undersized, two-person tables lined up opposite. Sliver tables. Here you eat cheek by jowl with strangers and must speak in low tones to avoid being overheard, while still unavoidably overhearing what is being said at the adjacent tables hard by your elbows.

Considerate restaurateurs provide plenty of room among tables and have no problem offering a four-top to parties of two if the place isn't packed. Further, if they're doing it right, they complement a spacious setup with comfortable chairs that sometimes might actually have arms. And at the bar, stools with backs. In such an establishment — where comfort is posited — the food will invariably be worthy, too.

NO GAMES. NO SHAMEFUL HUSTLE.

Next: Those skimpy wine pours, which these days are the norm, and are made all the more obvious by the use of huge wine glasses. In the name of allowing the wine to breathe and its "bouquet" to infuse your olfactory senses, restaurants use glasses big enough to hold a quart of milk. Into this tub they pour six miserable ounces, often pretentiously so from absurd mini-carafes as if they're pouring 1925 Lafite Rothschild. A serious drinker will dispense with six ounces in two healthy swallows.

This happens in fancy places, too, where a glass of wine might cost as much as 18 or 20 bucks, or even more, and yet still they feel no shame in beating you on both the price *and* the pour. Unfortunately, customers generally just take it, cowed into silence, just as they do when hearing about the Daily Specials.

Here, typically the server announces the specials, frequently in pedantic detail, though one important particular is often withheld—the price!—as if it's irrelevant. Worse, most people feel too embarrassed or intimidated to ask, which is precisely what restaurants intend. Imagine if the regular menu had no prices. (As the one for the lady used to.)

Absurd. But somehow, it's acceptable to withhold the price of the specials, and rely, again, on people being cowed into silence for fear of appearing inappropriately concerned about cost and insufficiently transported by the culinary experience so as to be indifferent to price. After hearing an elaborate recitation describing a dish in poetic detail, asking "How much?" sounds crass.

Nevertheless, if you should have the temerity to actually inquire, often the servers don't know. They know the special is garnished with parsley from southern Thailand and the sauce is a unique reduction prepared with mushrooms from the Peruvian mountains. But the price?

"I'll have to check."

What a crock!

Forcing people to choose between ordering an expensive dish without knowing its price and being embarrassed by inquiring, is plainly inhospitable. But because most people don't have the gumption to ask, or better yet complain, it's become the norm, not the exception, to withhold the price. Talk about uncool.

SERVER, DON'T BREAK OUR RHYTHM.

Restaurateurs with class are proud of their specials and transparent about the price. No games. No shameful hustle.

It isn't as if we all don't know that the specials will be the most expensive items, maybe $10 or $20 more than the highest-priced item on the printed menu. Hey, no problem. After all, they're supposed to be *special*, right? And, of course, we don't have to order them. Just don't make us have to ask "how much?" It's not nice.

One more thing. Server: there's a fine line between providing attentive service and blithely interrupting conversation. If you see that we're talking, don't break our rhythm for a perfunctory inquiry, or to press for additional orders. We know it's part of your job to try to lift our tab — just use common sense and proper timing. And remember, we're in a restaurant. We know how it works. If we need anything, we'll get your attention.

29

FREDDY THE FLEETWOOD

Fall 1973. I'm an East Coast expat newbie California lawyer living the dream in Berserkley, as we lovingly called it.

Earning $14,000 a year and feeling rich, wondering how I would spend it all — working for the long-gone Office of Economic Opportunity, which, before Nixon had his chums Rumsfeld and Cheney shutter the program, dispersed lawyers across the country to advocate for the poor.

Like a lot of others, however, I was preoccupied by the phantas-magorical counterculture smorgasbord that was rolling over us all. Encounter groups, transcendental meditation, yoga, psychodrama, food co-ops, Vietnam War protests, Grateful Dead concerts, free love — which, by the way, was never free; people were certainly promiscuous but there was a price to be paid — and yes, all manner of drugs.

There was, however, one major fly in the ointment. Gasoline. There wasn't any. Why not? Quick history lesson.

On October 6, 1973 (it was Yom Kippur, the holiest Jewish holiday), Syria and Egypt, with the support of other Arab nations, launched a surprise military campaign against Israel to regain territory lost in the June 1967 Six-Day War.

EVERYONE WANTED A SMALL CAR. ME INCLUDED.

A week later, on October 12, the U.S. resupplied Israel, and in response OPEC instituted an embargo on us and a few of our allies. Unbelievably, in those naïve times, there was no backup U.S. oil capacity. Gasoline quickly got very scarce, a situation that persisted for fully six months, until Nixon and Kissinger fatefully "persuaded" Israel to give up territory in the Sinai and Golan Heights in return for the lifting of the embargo.

But from October 1973 until March 1974, we waited in mile-long lines, sometimes pushing our cars the final 100 yards to the pump. And when we got there, we were limited to five, maybe 10 gallons.

Overnight, gas guzzlers were nearly worthless. Everyone wanted a small car. Me included. I bought a crappy little 1963 Fiat for $325. A complete shitbox. Cramped, noisy, powerless, which I had to park facing downhill in order to jump-start. But it got great mileage.

"LET'S GO SEE THE KING."

A great friend, William H. Elin (R.I.P.), was crashing at my $150/month rented house a mile or so from ground zero for those tumultuous times, the UC-Berkeley campus. One afternoon, he came back to the house and boldly announced:

"I bought a car today."

"Yeah. What'd you get?"

"It's out on the street. See if you can pick it out."

We go outside, I look up and down the street and see nothing that looks remotely like a candidate.

"Not a clue."

"How about the silver beauty right under that big nose of yours?"

"This whale?" pointing to a half-mile-long Cadillac parked curbside. "You're shitting me."

"Meet Freddy the Fleetwood. Look at it, cat! Vinyl roof, all leather interior, A/C, power locks, tilt wheel, cruise control, foot-controlled radio, eight speakers, safety sentinel, automatic dimming headlights, eight power windows including four vents..."

Then, opening the back door,

"And these gorgeous mahogany tables, which fold down from the back of the front seat with their own reading light. See! And the legroom! It's like a fucking hotel suite in here."

"How many miles on this tub, you lunatic?"

"28,000. It's cherry. This thing'll go 200,000, easy, even with the abuse we'll give it."

"What'd you pay for the beast?"

"Three hundred bucks. Less than you paid for that sick little Fiat of yours. Bought it from a recent widow intimidated by the gas lines. It's a 1967 Fleetwood Brougham ... a goddamn Michelangelo. Yeah, it gets lousy mileage, but I got it for next to nothing. We've got a cruise ship on wheels here, pal. Let's blast up to Reno. Elvis is playing at the Sahara. Enough with the fucking Grateful Dead. Let's go see The King."

OUR OWN MAGICAL MYSTERY TOUR.

And that's exactly what we did. Elvis's performance was never to be forgotten, and over the next few carefree years we cruised America in unmitigated splendor in Freddy. Our own magical mystery tour in the finest full-sized sedan ever to roll off the line in Detroit. An American classic, which my man bagged for a song because where everyone else saw gas lines, he saw a good time.

Now that, people, is what it means to think outside the box.

30

SATELLITE RADIO

In 2019, when I got my last car, it came with Sirius XM free for six months. So of course I used it and just as the bastards anticipated, got hooked.

I have come to especially love the really idiosyncratic channels like Radio Classics, which plays programming from the '30s, '40s and '50s, much of which, unfortunately, was well before my time. Abbott & Costello, Orson Wells, Jimmy Durante, Sherlock Holmes, Basil Rathbone, Our Miss Brooks, Dick Tracy, Boston Blackie, Dragnet, Burns & Allen, Jack Benny, and my favorite, Groucho. One classic after the next. A veritable feast.

As is the case today, these old radio programs provide a reliable window into the sensibilities of the times. The turn of phrase, the characters, the storylines, the heroes, the villains, even the commercials demonstrate how civilized and safe the world seemed "back in the day" (an example of using the phrase appropriately, referring to "a day" sixty, seventy, eighty years ago).

Even with World War II on the horizon, then in full conflict, and still later during the Cold War, there simply were no sharp edges to these radio shows. And certainly no profanity. Life was innocent. Almost halcyon. A family's big weekend outing was a Sunday drive in the country. Having an ice cream cone was a big deal. Playing hooky from school was as wild as kids got. Hell, the radio itself was only 30 years old.

LIFE WAS INNOCENT.

Listening to these old broadcasts transports us to a simpler, softer, safer, nearly unrecognizable time and place, almost as if we're visiting another planet.

31

CAR SEAT CREVICES

When is a car maker going to design seats that prevent our stuff from falling between the seat and the center console? This has been a problem since the appearance of the first bucket seats in the 1955 T-Bird.

LIKELY RECOVERING ONLY
A DECAYING FIG NEWTON.

For 65 years, keys, money, jewelry, food, and now phones have been disappearing into this grim abyss, requiring you to get out of the car, get down on all fours, move the seat up, move it back, root around blindly like a warthog to search for whatever you've lost, likely recovering only a decaying Fig Newton.

Where's the ingenuity?

The most favored current "solution" on the market is some half-ass, one-size-fits-all long foam cylinder that you jam into the crevice. It works, sort of, but really only underscores the need for the problem to be properly addressed by the manufacturers.

And don't tell me that because the seats move back and forth, and up and down, that the problem can't be solved. A competent graduate engineering student could design a solution in a week, maybe less.

32

JACKIE MASON

I'm driving down Central Park West in Manhattan. At the corner of 72nd Street I spot Jackie Mason, still hale and hearty at 91 in 2020, standing at the curb trying to hail a taxi.

HE LAUGHED OUT LOUD.

Notwithstanding his rightwing politics, Jackie's an old favorite of mine. His given name is Yacov Moshe Maza. He's an ordained rabbi, like his father, grandfather and great-grandfather, as well as all three of his older brothers. I'm also the youngest of four boys, so I always felt a connection with him (with Mel Brooks, too, also the youngest of four boys). I enjoy Jackie's wiseguy humor, typically one-liners like this classic on infidelity:

> "Eighty percent of married men cheat in America. The rest cheat in Europe."

Having just heard a cute joke I thought he might get a kick out of, I pull up beside him, power down the passenger side window and yell out:

"Jackie, what'd the little old Jewish lady say to the flasher as he opened his trench coat wide to expose himself?

"So what'd she say?"

"'You call that a *lining*?'"

He laughed out loud.

"That's funny. I'm stealing it."

"All yours, Jackie. I stole it too."

33

PROFESSOR HERBERT O. REID & COMMISSIONER LARRY O'BRIEN

Years ago, I had a particularly impatient although brilliant law school professor named Herbert O. Reid. Having been thoroughly put off by a rambling, specious soliloquy from one of my denser classmates, Professor Reid offered up this brutal approbation:

> "Sir, some of what you have said is important, and some of what you have said is correct. Unfortunately, the part that is correct is unimportant and the part that is important is incorrect."

Later, another student, seeking clarity on some issue or other, asked a question that began:

> "Is it true that...?"

Professor Reid taught constitutional law and having been co-counsel with Thurgood Marshall on the landmark desegregation case *Brown v. Board of Education* was keenly respected. Despite the definitive ruling achieved in that case, he nonetheless relentlessly preached that seeking certitude was a futile and unworthy pursuit. After a long, suspenseful pause, he responded to the "Is it true...?" query, exclaiming:

"It's true, sir, except if it isn't."

Meaning, of course, that the world turns. Things change. Certitude does not exist.

HE BECAME IMPATIENT WITH MY EXUBERANCE.

The importance of caution and restraint was similarly reinforced for me a few years later, when I was the young, ever-so-green executive assistant to NBA Commissioner Larry O'Brien. O'Brien had worked for both Presidents Kennedy and Johnson and been the intended target of the Watergate break-in when he was the chairman of the Democratic National Committee, from 1970 to 1972. Unknown to most, though factual, Nixon was seeking dirt on O'Brien from his time working for Howard Hughes, before he became chairman of the DNC. O'Brien was a hardened political operative with rarefied strategic acuity.

One afternoon I was celebrating having just convinced the famously irascible then-owner of the Los Angeles Lakers, Jack Kent Cooke, to pledge his vote to O'Brien on a particularly thorny issue to be taken up at an upcoming Board of Governors meeting. O'Brien, one of the most adept vote counters in the history of the Republic, was excruciatingly slow to count his chickens before they were hatched, and became impatient with my exuberance.

> "Careful, Bill. Remember, there are no final victories. Things unravel. Territory you conquer today can be lost tomorrow. Stop patting yourself on the back. Stay on the problem until the votes are cast. Then start worrying about a later reversal."

O'Brien's "No Final Victories" admonition (the title of his memoir), combined with Reid's "It's True Except When It Isn't" dictum, have informed my approach to business *and* life ever since.

Anticipate that the wind will change. Decrease the possibility of reversal by continuing to outwork the other side. There's always more to do. And if you do eventually win, *and* your victory is maintained, be quiet about it.

Gloating is for amateurs.

34

THE UPSIDE OF BEING WRONG

As you might suppose, being so opinionated, I'm not easily moved off positions I hold dear.

But there are certainly times when someone comes along with more experience, more insight, more candlepower, who turns a point of view of mine on its head.

REMEMBER, THERE IS NO EFFORT WITHOUT ERROR.

For a while, I don't feel so good. Dumb, mistaken, maybe even a bit lost. But hey, that makes sense, right? After all, I was *wrong*. Soon, however, I recover and feel better. Why?

Because I now understand my mistake and have gladly unloaded an old, tired, flawed notion which I've likely been lugging around and foisting on others, maybe for years. I'm carrying around one fewer misconceived idea. My load is lighter. I'm a little wiser and hopefully a bit humbler. By definition, I have experienced growth.

That's a deal I'll take every day and twice on Sundays.

"HMM.

INTERESTING!"

Remember, there is no effort without error. If you're not failing, you're not growing. As Hemingway advised:

> "The world breaks everyone and afterward many are strong at the broken places."

We're all wrong sometimes. We all fail. The trick is to fail fast and fail forward so that there's value acquired from the mistakes. Experience is simply the word we give our mistakes.

Success does *not* produce wisdom. Success grows confidence, but not wisdom. The truth is that the real winner in any situation is not the one who's right but the one who has had their world view expanded.

So when you make a mistake, when you stub your toe, don't just think,

"Ouch."

Also think:

"Hmm. Interesting!"

EPILOGUE

As I ready this collection for publication in the summer of 2020, it's impossible not to reflect on the coronavirus which continues to ravage the globe. Most any observation made now will in time be dated, but these, I expect, will stand the test of time.

IT'S HUMAN NATURE

Yes, there have been a multitude of mistakes, of both omission and commission, going back many years. Worse, when the pandemic struck, most countries reacted too slowly. Being late to a pandemic turns out to be a very bad idea. As they say, 90% of wisdom is being wise in time.

But before pointing fingers and railing about our, and the world's, lack of preparedness, before we launch volleys of recriminations, consider:

Fully 10 years ago, none other than Bill Gates warned that we were vastly unprepared for a future pandemic and called for governments to be ready to create, manufacture, and disseminate huge quantities of vaccines when the next one arrived.

Gates was ignored. Why? Why couldn't even Bill Gates stimulate serious action to improve our preparedness?

Here's why.

Events are seen differently depending upon the degree to which a person's, or a country's, self-interest is affected. The Spanish flu was too long ago to influence our collective self-interest, and none of the H1N1, SARS, MERS and Ebola epidemics spread globally. Now, however, having suffered gravely, we will be more prepared next time.

But we had to get hurt first. Until people get hurt, they don't act. Unfortunate. Sometimes catastrophic. Yet foreseeable. Throughout the ages, and now, too, people look the other way until their own ox is gored.

It's human nature.

A HEALED FEMUR

When calamity strikes, our ideas about civility and what it means to live in a civilized society get tested. Do most of us ever really consider anything, or anybody, beyond our own narrow worlds? How apt are we to meaningfully reach out to others in worse shape? These are questions which in normal times are largely thought exercises. Not now. Now, they test our core values.

For an anthropological perspective — often among the worthiest — we turn to renowned anthropologist Margaret Mead, who, it is said, when asked what was the earliest sign of civilization in an ancient culture, referred to a healed broken femur. She is reported as having continued:

> Such signs of healing are never found among the remains of the earliest, fiercest societies. In their skeletons we find clues of violence: a rib pierced by an arrow, a skull crushed by a club. But this healed femur shows that someone must have cared for the injured person — hunted on his behalf, brought him food, served him at personal sacrifice.

So there it is: the defining characteristic of civilized society is helping others. A critical reminder in these grievous times, and something that's not only transferable but empowering. That is, as the famous psychiatrist Karl Menninger instructed, there's healing power in helping others, illustrated by the story about a guy ready to jump off a cliff until someone else showed up at the same cliff ready to do the same thing, which motivated the first guy to reach out to the second and talk him out of it, and in the doing relieve his own despair. A win-win.

Stay safe.

Fall 2020

ACKNOWLEDGMENTS

A short book doesn't necessarily mean less work. As we know, less is often more. In this case, more work, for which I have the following people to thank:

Sarah Sheppeck, without whose steady hand *Skip the Funeral* would never have seen the light of day. Smart, committed, and always in good cheer, "Shep" has accommodated my ever-changing preferences while still managing to always drive this project forward.

Emily Browne, for her keen eye in crafting the look of this little epistle.

David Moran, who came in from the bullpen in the 9th inning to clean things up editorially. His rarefied expertise has improved all aspects of this project.

Ella Alber, my incomparable partner for 35 years, without whom whatever success I enjoyed in business would not have been possible.

My gifted wife, Deborah, who, having heard these ravings more times than anyone could be reasonably expected to endure, still managed to respond with forbearance and insight when asked to review it "one more time."

The "Sprout," my pistol-packin' daughter, Elizabeth, for her indefatigable spirit and authenticity.

Finally, Alan Finder, felled in March 2020 by the coronavirus. A friend for 55 years, and distinguished journalist, who over our many joyful lunches generously provided his seasoned counsel. Our world, my world, is sorrowfully diminished by his untimely passing.

ABOUT THE AUTHOR

Lawyer turned Sports Executive turned Storyteller/Observationalist.

After briefly practicing law in Berkeley, Bill opted out of a formal legal career and moved across the country to Manhattan in the improbable pursuit of a job in the world of sports. Following stints at Madison Square Garden and then the NBA, Bill and his partner, Ella Alber, co-founded in 1979 one of the industry's first sports marketing agencies. Over the course of the next 35 years, their company, Sports Etcetera, promoted over 1000 events worldwide while partnering with The Garden on the Virginia Slims Tennis Championships, which became the largest annual women's sports event in the world.

Presently flunking retirement and finally free from boardroom sensibilities, Bill has decided to scratch a longstanding itch and stop *hiring* the talent and *become* the talent. In addition to *Skip the Funeral*, his varying content can be found at www.billgoldstein.com and by listening to episodes of his podcast "Not That You Asked."